The Science of
Healthy Hair

The Science of Healthy Hair

Chuck Caple

Author of
Coloring Chemically Relaxed Hair

iUniverse, Inc.
New York Lincoln Shanghai

The Science of Healthy Hair

iUniverse books may be ordered through booksellers or by contacting:

iUniverse
2021 Pine Lake Road, Suite 100
Lincoln, NE 68512
www.iuniverse.com
1-800-Authors (1-800-288-4677)

Because of the dynamic nature of the Internet, any Web addresses or links contained in this book may have changed since publication and may no longer be valid.

The views expressed in this work are solely those of the author and do not necessarily reflect the views of the publisher, and the publisher hereby disclaims any responsibility for them.

ISBN: 978-0-595-45272-9 (pbk)
ISBN: 978-0-595-89587-8 (ebk)

Printed in the United States of America

Contents

THANKS, CONTRIBUTIONS & ACKNOWLEDGEMENTS

This project was made possible with the aid and assistance of some very influential people and human inspirations. First I must give hurrahs to my number one fans ... my number one supporters. I want to acknowledge that my wife Cathy and my daughter and son, Kwadena and Keanon continues to give me consistent encouragement to finish this project.

I want to give many credits to Devon Gossett of Dallas Texas. Devon is the master mind behind the industry changing technology that fueled most of this book. Devon is the President of Bac Stat Corporation and the spear head of the team of scientists out of Baylor Hospital in Waco Texas that developed this phenomenal technology that I introduce in the book. All of the photos and images and research introduced in this book is furnished to me by Devon. He has unselfishly provided me with this information.

I want to thank my team members of Marlene Freeman and Derron Carmichael, and Erica Carmichael who have become avid users of the technology that Devon and Bac Stat has provided. They have all used and experimented with the products and become frequent buyers.

I would also like to thank Roc Taylor of Dallas Texas who introduced me to Devon thus establishing a long and profitable relationship. Roc has become a supporter and admirer of mine and has had tremendous faith in the merger of Devon and I. Mr. Rodney Barnett of Dallas was also instrumental in the meeting of the two of us.

INTRODUCTION

Twenty two years after I walked through the first school of Barbering and Cosmetology, I press upon revolutionary breakthroughs in the industry of Hair Care as we know it. World changing progress has come upon us. If you find yourself in the core of this industry presently, then you have obligations that you'll find practically mandatory. I proclaim that you cannot consciously or morally stay in this industry and not invest or participate in the revolutionary technology that I'm about to present to you. The practice of relaxing and coloring as we see it, is about to change. The law of relaxing and coloring has been questionable at best. The principles and theories that supports these practices have been supporting and upholding through decades. These principles are universal and exclusive in its right. For some time now I've been questioning some of the principles of relaxing and coloring. I've came across numerous cases where exceptions have occurred during common procedures. To say the least, I've come to a conclusion that we sometimes have to approach each client as a "case by case" situation. The principles don't change but after years of servicing clients, there are more and more cases that defy theories. These documented discoveries that follows in the upcoming chapters will bring some clarity to the mysteries that we could never seem to understand. We as industry professionals have been tiptoeing through this industry with blindfolds or in sort of a mummy like state in the dark at the guidance and leadership of the many manufacturers and chemists who have mandated the pulse of things for so long now. We've been mere patients ourselves and the industry is our pharmacist prescribing the antidote for the day as we service the public. We never question our physicians who administer us drugs because we have reserved a certain level of trust. A trust synonymous to that is what we have developed in the industry of beauty. This level of trust establishes some extent of integrity in the industry but it really doesn't give us any merit or observation of the type of navigation that we should instill. I've always been passionate about information. Upon studying in preparation for this project, I compiled data and information that not only clarify many mysteries of this industry but it also questions the handling of information handed down by the manufacturers. I have no intentions of making any one particular source or group a scapegoat, but

I do relish the ability and opportunity to shed some industry breaking information to a group of "needing to know" professionals.

1

WHAT WE DIDN'T KNOW ABOUT RELAXERS

Relaxers have been providing the industry with a special service for decades. They seem to leave us few discrepancies because as far as most of us are concerned, they do exactly what they are supposed to do. The only problem is that we have not been versed enough in relaxer technology nor educated enough in relaxer theory to have ever been exposed to any abnormalcy. To put it simpler, the knowledge and research has never been presented to industry professionals before. You will all be blown away to know the real truths about what scientific research has turned up about relaxers. As far as the average stylist is concerned, the relaxers do an adequate or even excellent job of straightening the hair and there is no need to doubt its ability because they are satisfied with the results as well as the clients. They don't associate any damage or breakage with the relaxer. They identify damage with color, medicine, heredity etc. If the damage doesn't occur as a direct or immediate result from relaxer application, they attribute it to some other cause. Now here comes the startling truth about relaxers. Scientific research has established a reality that sets a whole different perspective on relaxing hair. Science has discovered through years of research that chemical relaxers (sodium hydroxide) has a unique characteristic that changes the theory of straightening hair. That characteristic is the fact that it fuses itself to the hair shaft and is never removed from the hair. I was attempting to explain this discovery to one of my clients and she said that she knew it. She thought she knew it but she really didn't. She couldn't have known it, because we as industry professionals didn't even know it until the scientists and doctors of chemistry had revealed it. My client was thinking of it in another sense. She was thinking of it in the sense that relaxers are permanent in its action and results, so therefore, it is not ever removed from the hair. That's also a true fact, but not the point that research is referring to. Sodium hydroxide fuses itself to the shaft and although the physical

1

product is rinsed from the hair, a film like deposit remains in the hair and is still working at decimal rates. Even though you cannot see it or actually feel it, the product is still in the hair. You can shampoo the hair a hundred times with a neutralizing shampoo or any other shampoo for that matter and it won't make any difference. You can even put neutralizing shampoo on the hair and place it under a plastic cap for an entire day and it won't do the trick. My client couldn't have known this. The stylist doesn't even know of this research because if they did, their actions and approach to straightening would be totally different. Now because this product is still in the hair, everything you do to the hair after is going to be a direct translation to any eminent danger or damage to the hair. The clients began to establish a regimen with the way they maintain their hair. They get retouches on a six to eight week basis, and color services two weeks before or after that. They also return to the salon for services that consists of hot curling and gel work. Keep in mind that your initial relaxer is still in the shaft and you continue to add more chemical each time you relax and sometimes that chemical may overlap. Now if you are overlapping, you are putting a double dose on the hair. A long cycle like this could definetly put the hair in harm's way. This is the factor that leads us into the initiation of breakage, damage and problem hair.

Another study and research showed that ph readings on many various relaxers displayed the surprising conclusion that there are differences in their strengths in relation to brands but not so much in relation to strength to strength. What do I mean by this? Well, study has shown that a mild relaxer for example varies in ph from one brand to another. One brand's mild formula may be different in activity according to ph than that of another mild formula from another brand. So when you create tendencies of switching relaxer brands on your clients with the presumption that one mild is the same as the other, then you may be misled. Every separate manufacturer's mild, normal or resistant formula is slightly different from its competitor. This is one reason why it is extremely important to keep consistency when servicing each individual client. On a separate note, study has also shown that contrary to what we have all been taught and what we've always believe to be true, there is not much difference in strength and activity from a mild to a normal. This could be a major factor in the reason why many recipients of chemical relaxers have been able to sustain the life of their hair with a normal relaxer while they are also recipients of permanent hair color. This however, does not mean that it is okay to do this and that there is no eminent danger of breakage or hair loss. Did you know that in the ingredients and the makeup of sodium hydroxide relaxers, there is only about two percent of sodium hydroxide present and the rest consist of buffers and conditioners? Well, this is very true. So when we think of the differences from mild relaxers to normal relaxers, we are not really speaking of vast differences. However, as I mentioned in my book, "Coloring Chemically Relaxed Hair", if you practice a service on one hundred clients and you have a ninety nine percent success rate, this means that it is not a fool proof service and is not one hundred percent safe. That's enough to say that maybe this is not a safe practice to keep. There is always that one percent chance that your next client may be the one whose hair may be compromised. All of these studies raise questions in the mind of researchers, educators and stylists alike. It questions the integrity of some of the chemistry in the products as well as some of the services that we have been rendering to our clients for decades. It doesn't necessarily question the product's ability to perform its duty but it does suggest that footnotes be added to the results that present themselves as a result of these particular services being applied to the hair. In other words, the principles and theories don't necessarily change but certain services do change the law of relaxing or coloring. This brings me back to my earlier statement that we sometimes have to approach each client as a case by case basis. Sometimes there are some exceptions to the rule. You're going to come across clients that won't respond positively to a service as another client would. Even there are going to be cases where a client's hair may defy all the rules and the theory. Some clients may totally reject theories and principles laid out by a certain practice. We know that a mild relaxer and permanent color are compatible and are safe routes to take. However, you may have a person who may be a mild relaxer client and be totally unreceptive to a permanent color. You may have a person who may be a normal relaxer client and receives permanent hair color well and be able to maintain the integrity of her hair as far as the naked eye can tell. So these are the instances that seems to suddenly make sense when we learn that relaxers and strengths vary but they are also the cases that makes us puzzled and causes us to question the theories that we have been basing our techniques and practices on for so long. So I say to you that as you read on further in this book, to keep in mind that our basis and principles we've entrusted all these years are still true and reliable but recent research presented by scientists and doctors of chemistry has proven that there are exceptions to each rule and when these exceptions come about, there is revolutionary study and revolutionary procedures that can be supplemented to your routine regimen that will preserve the integrity of your client's hair.

Chapter Review

- Relaxers fuses themselves to the hair and is never totally removed

- Neutralizing shampoos cannot stop the action of the relaxer in the hair

- Relaxer strength vary from one manufacturer to another

- One companies mild strength will be different from another

- Difference in activity from a mild to a normal or normal to a resistant is not very obvious. There is not much difference between each

- In the ingredients of sodium hydroxide relaxers, only about 2 percent is actually sodium hydroxide

- Most of the composition of the relaxers consists of conditioners and buffers

- This is why some clients with normal strength relaxers can endure permanent hair color

- Switching from one brand to another on the same strength does not mean they are the same strength in activity points

2

WHY HAIR BREAKS
(The Common Denominator)

Out of all the study that was done by scientists and doctors of chemistry, there is one research and finding that I am most fascinated with. I am going to share with the industry a very vital study of information that opens up the door to so much understanding and revelation to a problem that has been plaguing the industry and the business of hair dressing for as long as the profession has been in existence. We have had many explanations and reasons for hair breakage and hair loss for decades. Many experts and others have had their theories as to what makes the hair break. Some have said that strong relaxers damage the hair and causes breakage. Some have said that permanent color, bleach, cold waves, perms and thermal curling all have their part to play in breakage and damaged hair. All of these geniuses are correct. But there is a much deeper cosmetic look and reason for this problem. It is true that relaxers, perms, color, bleach, thermal curling and blow-drying all can cause damage, hair breakage and hair loss. The real question is: what characteristics of each of those services cause the damage?

Through this magnificent research and study done by the scientists and doctors of chemistry, we learned the one thing that helps us to solve all the problems that we've faced for so long. This research took place over an extended number of years. This study was done on various textures and nationalities of hair from African American, Caucasian, Hispanic, Asian and others. Years and years of study was done with these different cultures of hair and they were virgin samples of hair as well as samples that was treated with sodium hydroxide based relaxers, perms, bleach, color and heat services such as blowdrying and thermal curling. Every strand of hair in all the years tested turned up one common denominator. That factor was that the hair expanded. Not ninety nine percent or ninety nine and nine tenths percent but in every sample of hair tested with these particular services, there was one common characteristic. It all swelled. This study confirmed what was already known but never publicized in a national way. It confirmed that anything applied to hair of an alkaline state or any heat applied to the hair causes swelling. Now this is not brand new news or even revolutionary for that matter, but it is a known scientific fact. However, even though this fact has been known and even by some cosmetic chemists, it has never been taught to the industry professionals. I am speaking of the hair stylists. The reason why this information is not highly publicized is because there has been no real conclusive proven way or method of rectifying the swelling. There has been no technology in terms of products or cosmetic chemistry that totally reduced the swelling in the hair. Many may ask the question of why the swelling relevant to hair breakage or what is so distinctive about the swelling that we should be so concerned with. Well the swelling causes the breakage. As a matter of fact I would personally go so far as to say that the swelling of the hair is the one and only sole reason for the breakage in hair. You can quote me on that. I put my worthy name and reputation behind that statement. How can I be so assured of that? Some may say that leaving the relaxer on the hair too long causes damage in certain clients. Some say that too much bleach combined with developer causes it while others say that high level colors with a combination of high level developers causes damage. All of these culprits are correct. Even if you consider the heat from implements such as blow-dryers and curling irons as reasons for damage, you would still be accurate. Ultimately, all of these factors cause swelling. Therefore when the hair swells, it changes the porosity. It becomes more and more of a risk for continued swelling. When the hair is in a normal and healthy state it has elasticity and or the ability to stretch successfully without the risk of breaking. The more it swells the more danger it is in. The scientists use an analogy that explains it perfectly. They use a balloon as a symbol. Take a balloon and blow it up. Blow it up with about ten breaths of air. This balloon may be able to withstand up to twelve blows of air before it is in jeopardy of bursting. As long as you don't go any further than ten blows, you will be alright. However if you insert more than two additional blows of air, you are taking a chance of causing the balloon to burst. Hair is similar to the balloon. We relax or color the hair to a degree and cause a great deal of swelling in the hair and because we have had no real way of reducing the swelling the hair remains in a detrimental state. We then create a regimen that consists of us relaxing the hair on a six to eight weeks basis and coloring permanently on a schedule very similar to that of the relaxer service. Sometimes we overlap and we further inflict punishment to the hair by blowdrying and thermal curling. This is equivalent to taking that balloon and putting additional blows of air in it. So now we are continuing to add services to the hair that consists of techniques that causes swelling. Keep in mind that the previous swelling has not gone down and we continue to stretch the hair further. Now the porosity has changed tremendously and the elasticity has been taken to its limit. The hair has no where else to go at this point but to break. Anytime you put alkaline products on the hair you are increasing the swelling. Anytime you apply heat to the hair you are increasing the swelling. The main thing we want to be understood is that when you take the hair to these extremes, you have to revive it by reducing the swelling. You can condition the hair all you want and apply treatments accordingly but if they are not a contractor, then they will not prevent you from eminent danger in the future.

This is why I say again that the swelling is the sole and only cause of hair breakage. If you leave the strong relaxer on the hair too long and the hair becomes over processed it is causing the hair to swell. Yes the relaxer that is too strong in strength is the reason for the breakage but the only reason it did the damage is because it is in a high alkaline state and made the hair swell extensively. If the bleach with the developer is too much for the hair and caused it to snap it is only because the high alkaline characteristics made the hair to swell to dangerous levels and ultimately snapped as a result. If the high level color combined with the high level developer caused the hair to break it is only because the ammonia mixed with a fast acting and multiple activity points developer caused the hair to swell so much that it stretched beyond its elasticity level and tore in half. If you blow-dry and curl your hair daily and eventually you determined that it was the heat from the implements that damaged your hair, it is only because the heat gradually swelled the hair shaft a little each day until it had no where else to go. So you see, no matter what reason you can come up with for the breakage, it all reverts back to the fact that its characteristics were conducive to creating swelling. Scientific research over many years confirmed this with an overwhelming resounding one hundred percent testing analysis. This is why I am so resilient in my stance when I say that swelling is the one and only cause of breakage when it comes to chemicals and heat. Sure, simple every day common things like excessive and vigorous combing and brushing can snap the hair and cause breakage and shattered effected ends. I will refrain from saying split ends because as we learned from my book—"Coloring Chemical Relaxed Hair", split ends are only seen from a microscopic lens and not with the naked eye. So this validates all that I have been lecturing about for years. Make no mistake about it, you can take it to the bank. This is where your damage and breakage comes from. Until you develop technology that can reverse it, you have not reached the ultimate goal of Cosmetology and hair care.

Another sad and repulsive reality is that since the beginning of time, manufacturers and cosmetic chemists have not developed or discovered a method of solving this problem. We have been entrusting the performance of products for years, believing that they do exactly what they say they will do. Many of these products provide an adequate measure of conditioning and softening but are not capable or qualified to completely do what they say they can do. You may also find another alarming fact about your trusted manufacturers as well. They have been marketing and advertising products for years that are supposed to provide certain levels of protection for the hair that they have known was incapable of doing such. These are the only products and technology that we have been exposed to and the only ones at our resources. We put our trust in these products and we expect extreme results. We rely on it. Those of us who are passionate about our business, tend to convey our sincerity to our clients and we promote those products and technology in our consultations. We put our reputations on the line by standing up for these products. We have always followed the guidelines set by manufacturers because to tell the truth, we have no other choice. We have no alternative to stand by or to give opposition to the protocol that they put forth. Truth of the matter is, the stylists have no education that takes them into the realm or circle of chemistry and manufacturing. We have always followed the lead of the manufacturers and trusted that they know what they are talking about. Don't get me wrong. Manufacturers are not intentionally deceiving us. They don't set out to mislead or misguide us. They have been working with the best they have and providing us with the best information that they can give us. As I mentioned before, they have not been able to master the science of contracting the swelling caused by chemicals and heat. Neutralizing shampoos, conditioners and reconstructors all fit the bill of adequate and moderate conditioning but science has proven that they are no real solutions for contracting.

As I mentioned earlier, swelling occurs and does not contract on its own. The porosity is compromised and the hair remains in a debilitated state as a result of the swelling. All of the products that we have been accustomed to using thus far provide us with a limited amount of relief. Although the hair's health is still compromised, a little relief is given to preserve the stressed swollen hair. This relief is only temporary at best but it does allow for a little more life expectancy. Once that relief is exalted and cannot go any further, the hair is going to be broken. So in that respect, the manufacturers are giving us the best that is available to us.

Unfortunately, this is not enough. Therefore, being uneducated as we are to this issue, we continue to use the technology that is at our disposal. We can only use what we are exposed to.

My opportunity to work with scientists have defined the meaning of using chemical on the hair and cleared up the responsibilities of cosmetic chemists. Scientists have years of study under their belts and are required to write books before they can even be considered official. All of their work is based on pure science and not probability. Cosmetic Chemists have a degree in chemistry. They are worlds apart. The science and scientists behind these studies are versed and trained in the proficiency of alkaline and acid use in relation to chemicals and hair. These studies have been studied years before being released to the public world.

They have developed technology in the form of sound education and products that is the answer to all your damage and swelling problems. I'll take you into that technology soon but before we do that it is necessary to discuss a couple of other factors that is important in this complex industry of knowing and treating damaged hair.

Chapter Review

• There is one sole reason why hair breaks

• That sole reason is swelling

• There are many reason that attribute to swelling—alkaline based products and heat

• Relaxers, color and heat (blowdrying, heat implements such as curling irons, flat irons etc) causes swelling

• When the hair swells, it remains swollen

• Further stress and heat upon swollen hair will further swell it and snap it

• Bleach and relaxers left on the hair too long, implements that are too hot creates extreme swelling and breakage

• Swollen hair compromises and loses its elasticity

- No shampoos or conditioners are going to contract the swelling in the hair. The condition and soften but they don't stop or contract swelling

- Cosmetic chemists have a degree in chemistry

- Scientist's work is based on science, facts and years of writing books and editorials before becoming accredited

3

YOUR COLOR IS MISSING NOT CHANGED

Have you ever heard a client say to you that she has been relaxing her hair for years and never had any color in her hair but all of a sudden her hair has changed color? She will say that the relaxer has turned her hair color or has burned her hair. If you have been in the industry long enough you will come across this situation. Even if you are not a member of the cosmetology world, you may witness an individual that you notice a change in their hair color when they have not had a chemical relaxer. The reality of it all is that the hair has not changed color. Scientists have researched hair samples, treated with relaxers for years and has made a conclusive discovery. As you remember, I explained that chemical relaxers as well as colors, bleach, blowdrying and heat causes swelling of the hair shaft. A dramatic revelation takes place during this swelling process. Let's go back to the analogy that scientists use to describe swelling.

An example is made to show comparisons to what happens in relaxed hair. A balloon is used. This balloon is black in color. It is in a flat stage because it is not yet blown up. It is held up to a group of students that consists of licensed cosmetologists. It is acknowledged that the balloon is black in color. Now the balloon is blown up to about ten blows. It is then held up to the light. This blown up balloon represents the hair shaft that is swollen after a chemical service. As it is held up to the light, it is determined that it is slightly transparent now because you can see through it. Actually what is happening is that light is filtering through it because it is stretched to large proportions and its texture has changed. The same thing happens to the hair. The hair is swelled to extreme measures. Once it reaches this stage, light filters through it because it has expanded. It loses its elasticity and the porosity changes greatly. As it swells, color is minimized. The hair is stretched so much that the composition of black hair which are blends of red, starts to appear. So therefore, what you began to see is a filtering of light through the black hair which is visible reds.

Scientific research has proven this, and through studies at Baylor Hospital in Waco Texas; the microscopic images validated it. Through the help of electron microscopes, the hair was magnified one millionth of a decimal which is around the largest size the hair can be projected. At this level the hair was examined in its virgin state without any chemical services at all. The hair looked rough around the diameter of the cuticle and rugged along the edges but rather natural in the fact that it was not swollen. Then images were taken after the hair had been exposed to sodium hydroxide. The hair was swollen to a large degree and there was another intriguing characteristic about this sample. Not only was the hair swollen but it was also missing pigment. The hair seemed to be a deep reddish color throughout the entire shaft. Different degrees of relaxation showed different levels of missing pigment. This color was mild in appearance and it detected light flowing through it as it remained on the slide under the microscopic lens. This light shining on it gave it a sort of translucent appearance. This happened to the hair each time it was relaxed.

PREVAILING PIGMENT

As you are aware, the pigment in the hair goes through stages or levels as it is lifted out of the hair. When coloring the hair permanently with an ammonia based color, the hair goes through a decolorization process. This is the lightening or lifting of the pigment from the hair. During this process the hair goes through what is called a prevailing pigment stage. This stage is defined as the color that is left in the hair after lifting, but before depositing. There are ten levels of prevailing pigment. Among the first three stages or levels are: red violet, red and red orange. As you know, black is made up of a mixture that includes reds. Once the black is stretched and broken down of its density, it goes through a red stage or prevails to a red stage. This is what happens when that black hair is relaxed and swollen to a certain degree. It expands so much that it loses its density and is able to be seen through with the aid of light. So the relaxer is not changing the color of your hair and the ingredients in the relaxer are not burning the hair to the degree that it is physically turning it colors. It just swelled the hair to the extent that a filtering of light passed through it.

When the scientists performed the last test on the relaxed hair it returned to its original state. Microscopic photos showed the hair being returned to its original

Your Color Is Missing Not Changed 13

state. When it was returned to its natural state, not only was the swelling gone but the color returned as well. This study proved that when the hair seemed to have changed colors and remained that way, it was never returned to its original state by a means of contraction. That hair remained that way because until now there was no real way to contract it. This hair as we know it, would then go on to be susceptible to being snapped, split or broken ultimately due to its minimized state of porosity.

Manufacturers, chemists and product makers have never explained this situation to the stylists and industry professionals so we have no real conception of what is going on and therefore we pass this mystery on to our clients. Up until recently we all thought that the hair was actually changing color due to the presence of the relaxer. We acknowledged that those certain clients never had a color before and that the relaxer had to be the only reason for the color change. There was no explanation to be given by the manufacturers because they had none and there was no methods developed to revert that change in color. Therefore, the circumstances continued.

Now there are those clients who say that their hair has been subjected to the same kind of transformation and that they don't have a chemical in their hair. One may ask how does this take place without the presence of a relaxer. As I mentioned earlier, chemical relaxers are not the only culprit to creating swelling of the hair. Anything of a alkaline state and any type of extensive heat can create just as much swelling as a relaxer. Heat can cause similar damage but in a much slower developmental phase. Curling irons, blowdryers and any other heat implements causes swelling when used in a repetitious manner or frequent routine. This swelling is the same and the results are equal even though it may take twice as long to occur. A client who is relaxer free can stand twice as much heat services as a client who has a relaxer, but will incur equal damage over a much extended period of treatment. Keep in mind that even though the weapon is heat as opposed to chemicals, the swelling is permanent unless you have the technology to reverse it. Therefore, the swelling continues to increase with each service and the pigment is altered visually because of the filtration of light that passes through it.

The alarming conclusion to this long time mystery is that when the hair is swollen or stretched to the point of altering the color, it is at the point of unreturned healthiness. When the hair reaches this stage it is already pushed so far on the alkaline side of the ph scale that it has lost all elasticity and tensile strength. This hair has had its integrity compromised extensively and is doomed for severe breakage. It is only a matter of time at this point before the inevitable is destined to happen.

Chapter Review

- Relaxers don't change the color of the hair

- What you witness is a flitration of light through swollen hair

- Hair returns to natural color and state when contracted

- A change in color from black to the reds as in prevailing pigment is similar to what happens when a color change is perceived from relaxing

- When the hair is stretched extensively the black thins out and it's underlying makeup is shown when light is filtered through it

- Color is not changed but because black consists of reds, it appears that it has changed when the hair is stretched

4

UNDERSTANDING THE PH SCALE

The ph scale has always been a tool of mystery to me and one not with complete clarity to it. Up until now I have had minimal comprehension about it and limited ability to convey the teachings of it to my audiences over the years. After in depth study with the scientists on the subject of ph, it has brought a lot of clarity to what actually happens to the hair when mixed with any solution whether it be water, conditioners, chemicals etc. My attempt now is to enlighten all my readers and followers so that this proficient tool will bring to light a lot of understanding that so many mysteries have presented.

The ph scale explains many things about many aspects of this industry. Let's begin. First let me begin by explaining as shown in the illustration below that the ph scale ranges in activity from 1 to 14. Seven is the neutral point. Everything below seven is considered acidic and everything above seven is considered alkaline. In the diagram below (figure 4), the scale illustrates where your products and chemicals are situated.

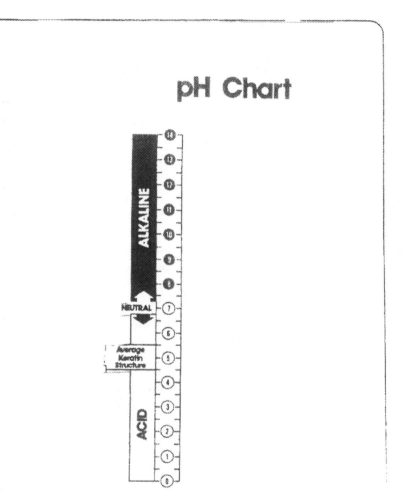

Your shampoos are normally around 6.0 and 7.0 and slightly higher. Your colors are formulated around 9.5 to 10.0. Your straighteners are formulated around 11.5 to 14.0 and your perm solutions are around 8.5 to 9.5. The hair and skin is acid balanced around 4.5 to 5.5. Most of your neutralizing shampoos are formulated around 5.5 to 6.0. Now here is where all of this becomes relevant to the industry professional. In my sessions with the scientists, I was taught the relevance and significance of the scale. They (scientists) read the scale in what they call a logarithmic procedure. Every point on the scale has ten times the activity points as the previous point. The diagram below illustrates the sequence and the breakdown of the activity points. Read with me and examine the scale as I explain its meaning and purpose.

pH Chart

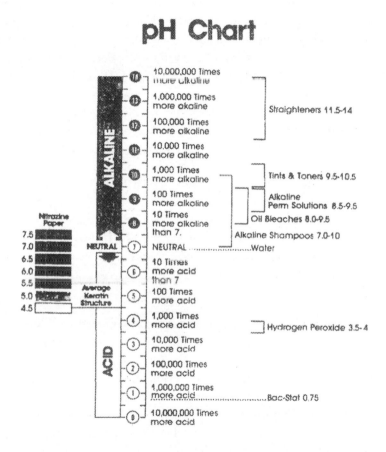

Seven is the neutral point or zero as the scientists like to put it. Everything thing above seven is alkaline. Eight has ten times more activity points as seven. So ultimately, eight has ten (10) activity points. Nine has ten times the activity points as eight which is one hundred (100). If this is too complicated to understand, just understand that we are multiplying each step of activity by ten. So nine has ten times the ten activity points that eight had which makes it one hundred. Ten on the scale has ten times the activity of nine which is one thousand (1000). Eleven has ten times the activity which is ten thousand (10,000). Twelve has ten times the activity that eleven has which is one hundred thousand (100,000). Thirteen has ten times the activity as twelve which makes it one million (1,000,000). Fourteen has ten times the activity points as thirteen which would make it ten million (10, 000,000). The same principle applies to the other side of the ph scale. Six has ten activity points or ten times more acid than seven and it ends up at one, with ten million. These numbers will have no significance if you don't remember where each one of your products come in on the scale. Keep in mind the location of the products that I explained earlier in the chapter. Let's discuss the chemical relaxer as it would pertain to the ph scale. The relaxer as we mentioned has a characteristic that causes it to fuse itself to the hair. It becomes permanent for all intents and purposes. Based on scientific research, the relaxer never leaves the hair. It cannot be removed with a neutralizing shampoo. Contrary to what we have been taught over the years, it cannot be done. Sodium hydroxide cannot be removed and it is dangerously working inside the shaft at decimal rates. The only way for the sodium hydroxide to be removed from the hair, it has to be turned into a sodium chloride (table salt) first. This can only be done with technology extensive enough and strong enough to accomplish it. Unfortunately until now, there has never been any technology or product worldwide that could accomplish this. The scientists that I have been working with have developed such technology.

Now before we go any further, I realize that many of you reading this will ask the very important question of why a neutralizing shampoo won't remove the relaxer from the hair. As I mentioned, a relaxer in the form of a sodium hydroxide has to be converted into a sodium chloride (table salt) before it can be removed from the hair. This can only be done with a product or another chemical strong enough to do so. Scientists have determined that this chemical can only be counteracted if it have another chemical equal to its strength. Let me explain how this matters and how it makes sense in relation to the ph scale. As we know, a neutralizing shampoo is formulated consistently around 5.5 to 6.0 on the ph scale. Some shampoos vary. Please keep that in mind. However, these shampoos generally have between ten and one hundred activity points on the acidic side. Manufacturers have been telling the industry for decades that these products will kill the actions of chemical relaxers. In all honesty, these shampoos characteristically bring the high leveled alkaline hair back into an acid environment, thus removing it from the alkaline state. The characteristic of these shampoos is to stop the chemical action and remove the product from the hair so that it can be neutralized or diminished to the point of normalcy and safety. This is what we have always believed to be true. We never questioned the accuracy of it or even questioned whether or not it actually stopped the relaxer from working. It was our place and position to trust in the products and the makers of the products that we used and not be bothered with whether or not they were adequate. We knew we had a core of professionals designated to deal with those concerns and all we had to do was to go to work.

Meanwhile, we go back and consider where our relaxers are on the ph scale. These chemicals are formulated around 13, 13.5 and up to 14 on the scale. If you refer back to your diagram provided for you earlier in this chapter, you will see that these chemicals have at least one million activity points on the alkaline side. Based on the discoveries and findings of the scientists, in order for neutralization to take place, the chemical doing the neutralizing would have to have at least equal activity points in the opposite direction of the alkaline chemical. We established that commercial neutralizing shampoos have about ten to one hundred activity points. This is not a sufficient strength of chemical to remove a sodium hydroxide or strong enough product to convert this sodium hydroxide into sodium chloride. I like to use an example of a tug of war. You have one million individuals standing on one side of a body of water with a rope. On the other side of that body of water you have one hundred individuals. The probability of those one hundred individuals pulling one million individuals into the water is impossible. No chance exists of this happening at any time. This holds true with the relaxer and the neutralizing shampoo. There are simply not enough activity points to even come close to solving the problem. This revelation educated me on something even more benefiting to my practice. I have done research and found many of these neutralizing shampoos are formulated the same as your normal conditioning shampoos on the market. This establishes that these distinctly different shampoos have the same number or level of activity points. During this study, I am understanding more and more each day that a lot of the products we use on a daily basis is designed as a marketing strategy and a means and way of making more money for the companies. In essence, the neutralizing shampoo is pointless. It is meaningless in my opinion. It has no real basis and no real responsibility. Why should you spend hard earned money on these types of shampoos when you can just as easily purchase a regular conditioning shampoo and accomplish the exact same thing. Manufacturers would probably imply that a neutralizing shampoo is a necessity because it contains exclusive ingredients that are designated for removing the relaxer from the hair. They would probably insist that your normal conditioning shampoo is not sufficient as well. Information of this source would be considered controversial and threatening to the welfare of many of the manufacturers' product life. They would never concur to this and would not agree that such information is true. They have been supplying the industry for years with products that has made this industry what it is today and at the same time they have managed to deceive us with select technology that has no real significance to the building and preserving of the hair's integrity. Some of this deception and neglect has not been intentional but merely an inability on the manufacturer's behalf to have the resources to deliver what they actually advertise. This is just a shortcoming on their part. They have actually been advertising and marketing their ability to treat, protect, build and correct problems and areas that they really weren't capable of accomplishing. None of the industry professionals have ever been in a position to contradict what the manufacturers suggest or ever had enough education on the subject to suggest otherwise. So instead of giving us the real story, they continue to promote hair growth, reconstruction and everything else when they knew that there was no real proof.

Now you have insight on the validity of the neutralizing shampoo. Don't get me wrong when I say that the neutralizing shampoo is inadequate when it comes to removing the chemical relaxer. Your regular conditioning shampoo is just as inadequate as well. It is not any more equipped in removing the sodium hydroxide from the hair either. As I mentioned earlier, it has about the same level and number of activity points as the other. It is the procedure that follows that makes the difference. The low ph level technology that you use on the hair after the shampoo is the difference maker. Using a normal shampoo instead of a neutralizing shampoo is an economical decision and choice and is more practical in the sense of arriving at a mutual or similar point. Now you have a multi purpose shampoo. One that cleanses and conditions the hair and also removes traces and deposits of relaxer from the hair adequately enough to be considered a neutralizing shampoo. You're killing two birds with one stone now. Manufacturers made decisions and practices for years with economic goals and now you're doing the same thing but with a different angle.

Chapter Review

• Scientists reads the ph scale in what they call logarithmic procedures

• 7 is considered neutral

- each point on the scale has ten times the activity points as the previous or can be read as ten to the tenth power

- everything below 7 is considered acidic

- everything above 7 is considered alkaline

- each point below or above 7 is read as follows: 10, 100, 1000, 10,000, 100,000 & 1,000,000 in terms of activity points

- relaxers are formulated around 13 and up on the scale/this gives them about 1,000,000 activity points

- neutralizing shampoos are formulated normally between 5.5 and 6.5 on the ph scale/this gives them around ten to 100 activity points

- the only way a chemical with a million alkaline activity points can be removed is if another chemical with equal activity points in the opposite direction is used (acidic activity points)

- sodium hydroxide has to be turned into a sodium chloride (table salt) before it can be released from the hair

- neutralizing shampoos does not have enough activity points to remove a chemical relaxer

- a regular shampoo that conditions and is formulated the same as a neutralizing shampoo is equally adequate for shampooing after a relaxer service and more economical

- your colors are formulated around 9.5 to 10.0

- a neutralizing shampoo is practically pointless

5

WORLD CHANGING TECHNOLOGY

As we discussed in the previous chapter, the neutralizing process provides us with limited abilities. Please keep in mind that I am not suggesting that the neutralizing shampoo does not cleanse the hair of traces of sodium hydroxide or any other chemical relaxer. I am merely stating that while it may cleanse traces of product, it does not resolve the problem or issue of the remaining chemicals inside the shaft that may be working or existing in a living sense at decimal marks. I have concluded however, that the use of this particular product serves me no purpose anymore and I've decided to limit my number of different shampoos. Some that is supposed to neutralize can also cleanse and some that can cleanse can also neutralize. I want this information to be enlightening and educating. I am not instructing anyone to discontinue purchasing neutralizing shampoos from their designated companies. My intentions are to inform you and the decisions you make in reference to such, is yours and only yours. You have an option. We never knew that there were options before now. In my opinion it is easier and more economical to use one shampoo for dual purposes. You may or may not feel the same way.

In further working with this team of scientists, they have given me the key to a lot of questions and concerns about removing the chemical off of the hair. As I mentioned earlier, there has to be a transformation of sodium hydroxide into sodium chloride in order to be a complete removal of relaxer from the hair. I also mentioned that in order to do that, a chemical equal in strength in the opposite direction is required as well in order for this transformation to take place. Since a neutralizing shampoo is not sufficient to do this, there had to be a product or system that could. Until recently there has not been any technology that was designed or created that was strong enough in activity points to make this happen. No manufacturer or company had developed such technology or they had not been scientifically equipped to do so. I'm not even sure if there has been any conception or indication on the manufacturer's part that this process was even possible or whether or not they even knew that such scientific approach would be the answer. As I stated earlier, contraction of swelling was the solution but there had been no invention as to how this contraction could take place.

During earlier times there was a product that was introduced to the United States from Belgian by a gentleman affiliated with this team of scientists that was formulated around 2.0 on the ph scale. This product was the only product close to the number of activity points needed to diminish the chemical action but it still wasn't strong enough. These scientists who had some individuals that were at some point in time working in aerospace, were quite fluent in the language and understanding of acids and alkaline. This put them in an environment that separated them from all others in the understanding of what was needed to make this world changing accomplishment. They developed technology that would have enough activity points to combat the high level of activity created by the sodium hydroxide relaxers. They knew they had to formulate this potion around 1.0 on the ph scale for it to even register to being adequate enough. Initially, they had developed this product at about .75 on the ph scale. During the development they determined that the product was too strong and it was irritating the skin. This product however was considered to be thousands time stronger than battery acid. Even though this was true, expert development and their abilities as scientists enabled them to construct the formula so that it would be acceptable, approved and tolerable to the skin. At this point, they had to revise the formula and bring it up to a 1.0 on the scale.

Now what does this product do? Well, it treats the hair after relaxing and allows the contraction of swelling to take place that is needed in order to return the hair to its virgin like state. Below you will see microscopic images of the hair in stages from virgin to relaxed to swollen to contracted.

BLACK HAIR — VIRGIN

This image illustrates virgin black hair. You can see that it looks fairly normal in size and complex with the exceptions of a little roughness along the edges. This is how the hair looks before any chemicals have been applied.

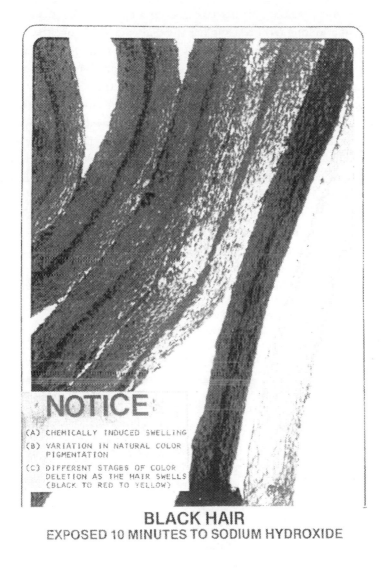

(A) CHEMICALLY INDUCED SWELLING
(B) VARIATION IN NATURAL COLOR PIGMENTATION
(C) DIFFERENT STAGES OF COLOR DELETION AS THE HAIR SWELLS (BLACK TO RED TO YELLOW)

BLACK HAIR
EXPOSED 10 MINUTES TO SODIUM HYDROXIDE

This illustration shows how the black hair looks after having a sodium hydroxide applied to it for a period of 10 minutes. As you can see, the hair is swollen to massive degrees and there has been a distortion or altering of color in the shaft. If you can remember, we discussed an analogy of a balloon in chapter 2. What's happening here in this illustration is exemplary of that explanation. The hair has swollen so much that the stretching has caused light to filter through it, thus giving it the illusion that the hair has changed colors. Often times, women think that consistent and long term relaxing has the tendency to change the color of the hair. Relaxing is the only foreseeable reason why the hair would change colors without the application of an artificial color process. This however, is a mistruth. The hair has stretched so much that when held against the light it appears to have changed colors. This is merely a filtration of light that passes through the hair. This swelling that you see in this illustration has until now been irreversible as far as the manufacturers developments have been concerned. This same swelling you see here remains in this altered state and only get worse with continued and added re-touches, color and heat. So you see, without correction or the contraction of this swelling the hair stays like this. If nothing is done to reduce or stop this type of swelling, the hair is bound to suffer damage or breakage should anything remotely strenuous is done to the hair. The scientists knew this and could see the swelling and the eminent damage from further dressing the hair so they developed this technology and product to reverse it. Here is another image that will show you how the hair looks after being relaxed and then treated with this industry changing technology.

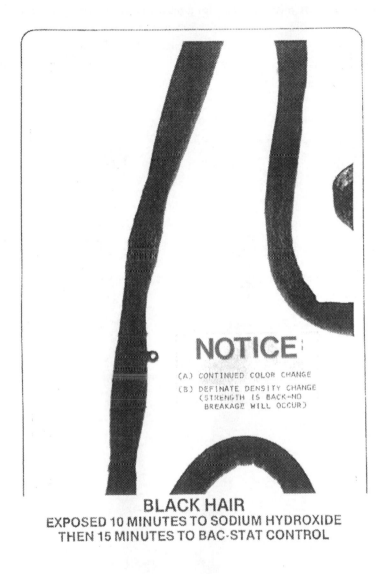

BLACK HAIR
EXPOSED 10 MINUTES TO SODIUM HYDROXIDE
THEN 15 MINUTES TO BAC-STAT CONTROL

This image is the same hair strands that you saw in the previous illustration but now it has been treated for 15 minutes with the 1.0 ph contractor. As you can see it has reduced the swelling considerably and is almost back to its original size. You will also notice that not only has the swelling gone down, but the hair has returned to its original color. Keep in mind that as long as the hair is not swollen, it has elasticity. This means that as long as it has elasticity, it has the ability to stretch. All the swelling that you witnessed in the photos above left no room for the hair to stretch. If any stretching took place, it would have caused the hair to snap or break. This contraction brings the swelling down but the hair remains in a relaxed and straight configuration.

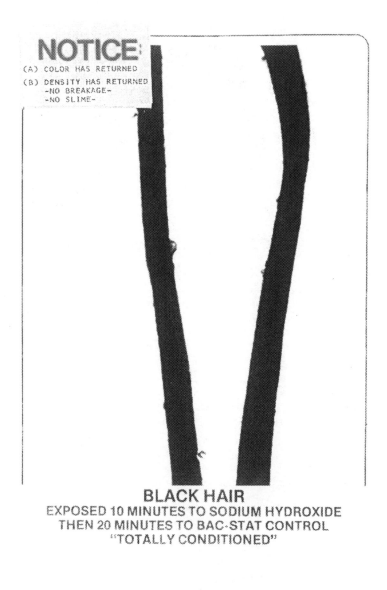

NOTICE:
(A) COLOR HAS RETURNED
(B) DENSITY HAS RETURNED
    —NO BREAKAGE—
    —NO SLIME—

BLACK HAIR
EXPOSED 10 MINUTES TO SODIUM HYDROXIDE
THEN 20 MINUTES TO BAC-STAT CONTROL
"TOTALLY CONDITIONED"

This image shows the hair after being treated and exposed to 20 minutes of the 1.0 ph product. The hair is totally conditioned and has returned to its virgin like state. This is the only product and technology of its kind.

How does this product work and how is it administered? After relaxing the hair, a complete and thorough rinsing of the hair is required. Shampoo the hair thoroughly and completely twice. After rinsing the shampoo from the hair you will then apply the product to the hair. If the relaxer is a re-touch application, you need to use on the new growth area only unless a conditioning or treating of the shaft is needed. Simply separate the hair with your fingers to expose the scalp area where the relaxer had been applied. Spray a thorough mist of product in those areas ensuring that you cover all relaxed areas. This product has tendencies to leave the hair a little raspy and rough so a combination of the contractor and a moisturizing conditioner is recommended. This will allow the hair to be soft and manageable while still being treated successfully with the contractor. Cover the hair with a plastic cap and place the client under a pre-heated dryer. You can cut your drying time down with a dryer or if you prefer you can simply let the client sit.

This product is not only for treatment following relaxers. You can use this product immediately after coloring the hair as well. It is also used on the hair before styling if the client has damage involving shedding, breakage etc. Permanent hair coloring as well as some temporary hair coloring swells the hair and needs to be contracted as a result. This technology comes in handy and as a great factor in preserving the health and integrity of the hair. The hair goes to great lengths of swelling with permanent hair color just as they do with relaxers and that particular swelling is no different than the other. Neither one contracts on its own and loses more elasticity with further chemical processing. Remember that any breakage and damage is either a direct or indirect result of some type of swelling of the hair shaft which means that the administering of this technology is going to be beneficial. In other words, this technology is great treatment for any type of damage and is great as a corrective source for many damage problems.

Chapter Review

- the swelling contractor is formulated at 1.0 on the ph scale

- this contraction product has about 1,000,000 activity points on the acidic side

- this product is compatible or comparable to diminishing sodium hydroxide and turning it into sodium chloride (table salt)

- when the hair is relaxed chemically it swells to major proportions

- the hair takes on the illusion that it changes color

- actually light filters through the hair because of how much it swelled and does not actually change colors

- swelling does not go down on its own

- contracting product is the only product in the world that can reduce the swelling from relaxing

- after 10 minutes of treating with the contraction technology, the hair shrinks back down considerably

- hair loses elasticity when swollen

- contraction product brings back the elasticity

- contraction product also brings back the original color

- after 20 minutes of treatment, the hair returns back to its virgin like state

- this product can be used equally affective with color and any other damage created services

6

BREAKING ALL THE RULES

With this introduction of technology comes a whole new approach and attitude toward standards and the way we look at the industry. We have protocols that we have followed since the beginning of time in the industry as it pertains to relaxing, coloring etc. These protocols are not just there because of rules or standards but because of principles and theories. We don't relax hair for lengths of 45 minutes to an hour because it's the rule, but more so because it's not safe or healthy. We don't permanently color relaxed hair with 40 volume peroxides because it's not safe as well as the theories and principles that go along with it. However, the technology that was introduced in the previous chapter is a parameter setter for many aspects of the business. It changes guidelines and borders for many different practices in the industry. It resolves one main and major issue involving preserving the hair and because of its responsibilities it affects how we do everything else under the umbrella of hairdressing.

Let's look at one critical and controversial issue in hairdressing. For decades or longer, the rule of thumb is that you cannot and should not chemically relax hair and permanently color it in the same day. We have known this for some time now. We know the repercussions that come along with this kind of practice. It is a sure fire way to hair loss and hair breakage without a doubt. One of the many warnings you get fresh out of beauty school is not to relax and permanently color in the same day. Some of us don't do it because it's ultimate rule. Some of us don't do it because we know better and or we've had the experience that comes along with having done it. Regardless, it is a practice that all African American salons stay away from as well as any other culture of salon that chemically relaxes hair. We just don't do it. Now all of that has changed. Let me explain.

We know that the hair contractor technology takes the swelling out of the hair. We also know that once this contraction takes place, the hair is in a much healthier state. It is also in a much less chance of damage and breakage. We know that with this contraction, the hair's elasticity is restored to its original state. Once this restoration of elasticity takes place the hair is no longer in danger or risk. Hair that is in no risk is hair that is a good candidate for whatever treatment or service you desire. When the hair is this healthy your percentage of damage is minimal. This is why we treat the hair with this technology because we want the hair to be as strong as it possibly can be. Now the subject of relaxing and coloring comes into play. We have known for a while that those two services are not meant to be mixed. However, we have this new technology. Now we can go ahead and relax the hair chemically. After this service, it is understood that the hair has gone to great lengths on the alkaline side. Its integrity has been compromised extensively. You've just put a chemical on the hair that has the vicinity of one million activity points. You also know that the hair has gone through some extensive swelling. If you refer back to the illustrations in chapter 6 you will be reminded of how much swelling takes place. The hair is in a weak state at this point. It is very vulnerable and any close proximity of stress to this already stressed hair could push it over the top. It is obvious that this hair needs to be treated and brought back to a safe level. It is not advisable to stress this hair any more at this point, not even for something as simple as blowdrying. So we have to treat the hair. The contraction technology is now used on the hair to bring it back to its safe and virgin like state. You can't see it with the naked eye but it is taking place. After about 20 minutes of treatment with the contraction process, the hair has regained its elasticity. It is also in a virgin like state as it was before relaxation. This means that the hair is no longer in jeopardy. It is no longer in danger of being stressed, stretched or snapped because of swelling that took place during the relaxation process. So if the hair is in a virgin like state and has full range of its elasticity, shouldn't it be safe to proceed with a color? Well the answer is now yes. Before, this would be unquestionable. This would be unheard of. The hair is as if it was never relaxed. It can be stretched as if it hadn't already been stretched. Of course the hair is going to be swollen all over again now because you are putting a chemical on it that has about one thousand activity points. You have now returned the hair to a weakened state. Just as you treated the hair after relaxing with the contraction process, you will have to repeat the service. Repeating this will once again return the hair back to its original healthy level. I suggest that you start a regimen of treatments on future visits to the salon as a precautionary measure after services such as this.

Keep in mind the lessons we learned in my previous book, "Coloring Chemically Relaxed Hair". We don't want to steer away from good practices and good habits.

You want to continue to relax the hair in the manner in which I discussed and continue to use the mild relaxer theory as a rule of thumb. We know that we can relax any head of hair with mild relaxer and not only that but it leaves your color door open. This means that with the mild relaxer it is the safest measure to take when considering permanent color down the road. Now with your mild relaxer, you can color it the same day as long as you use the contraction process introduced in the previous chapter.

This process kind of breaks all the rules. However, I feel that it is vital that I stress that there are always exceptions to the rule. By this I mean that you have to examine and analyze each head as an individual case by case situation. Some of those heads may have issues that raise questions as to whether or not this practice can actually be done. If a specific client has hair that is already thin and small in diameter, fragile in tensile strength or light in density, then you may want to reconsider this type of service. If a client has a history of damage or problem hair, you have to use your professional judgment about whether to proceed with a service such as this one. Therefore, please do not misinterpret my text and think that just because of the new technology that any recipient is a good candidate for having their hair relax chemically and permanently colored the same day. There are many factors that have to be considered in cases like these. So again, you have to be mindful of the type and strength of relaxers you are using and the makeup of color that you are using. Certain developer levels and content and level of ammonia have to also be considered when combining the two on the same day. Careful application of the contracting formula has to be administered as well. When you apply a relaxer to the hair in a re-touch manner it is important to know that the areas near the scalp where the relaxer was applied is the concentrated areas for the formula. Over saturating serves no real purpose. I suggest, recommend and instruct you to spray the formula at the scalp area and to separate the hair with fingers to insure that all areas of relaxation has been reached. On the other hand, when the color is applied following the relaxer, it is important to pay close attention to where the product is placed. If the color is applied in a re-touch manner then the same rule applies as the relaxer. The contracting formula needs to be applied at the scalp. If the color is applied in a virgin application technique then the contracting formula needs to be applied all over the shaft from scalp to ends and done in a way that all hair is covered. This should be done the same way with the fingers shifting through the hair making sure all the hair is covered but not in a manner that too much product is used and the hair is over saturated and soaked. Too much formula can be retro active. One thing I mentioned in previous chapters that I feel should be re-established is that while all this treating of the hair is strengthening the hair and restoring the hair, there is also conditioning issues that should not be overlooked. This contracting service is an excellent source of new technology that we've needed for so long, but you also have to remember that the hair is acquiring a rough and raspy feel. Each time you treat the hair with this, you are putting a rough feel to the hair so you have to continue to add a softening conditioner to the product to ensure that the hair is maintaining its great feel. So to say the least, it is wise to say that proper consultations and intense and extensive analyzing of the hair is key to successfully conquering this service and maintaining the hair's strength and integrity. In conclusion, I would say to the stylist to not ever rush in haste to clients desiring these services simply because it may finally be able to be accomplished. Don't always assume that it is for everybody. Consult and analyze!

There is another big concern of many professionals in the business today that I would like to address and explain how this new technology contributes to it. We always had desires and wishes of speeding up our processes in the salon because time is a major factor and we want to make as much money as we possibly can. Spending too much time on one client has been a stickler with many of us. How can we cut down on the time you may ask? Here's how you can approach this issue. Let's look at it from a hair color standpoint. We know that when permanently coloring hair it is mandatory and standard to process the hair a minimum of 45 minutes or you run the risk of under processing the hair and your color may not be completely developed. To many clients as well as stylists, this is entirely too long. However, it is necessary. Let's examine the processing time. If you leave the client sitting in the chair uncovered with her color it will process at room temperature which is about 72 degrees. This will successfully process the hair at 45 minutes. You can cut that time down to about 22 minutes by placing that client under a plastic cap which will change from room temperature at 72 degrees to about 94 degrees. This cuts the processing time down considerably. Or should I say speeds up the processing time. Now for those of you whose time is so valuable and you need to move even quicker than that, we can now put that client under a hooded dryer. By putting that client with a plastic cap under a dryer, you are now moving her from a processing temperature of 94 degrees to about 112 degrees. By doing this, you are cutting the time down from about 22 minutes to about 12 minutes. The heat from the cap and the dryer and the body temperature has now cut your processing time down to about 12 minutes. Keep in mind that the permanent hair color is not only swelling the hair with large numbers of activity points but the addition of the heat from the cap and the dryer is increasing the activity points as well. Now you have to finish it off by treating the hair with the contracting product which will bring the hair back down to a safe level. You see, this can indeed be done but you have to make sure that you have sufficient methods of returning the hair to a safe level in the end. No conditioners out there and no other treatments out there is going to accomplish the contracting needed except for the technology I introduced in chapter VI. The other conditioners traditionally used will do an adequate job of softening and possibly aligning but none of them will reduce the swelling caused by the activity of the color and the heat. So you see, all the things that we have been so accustomed to doing all these years that are damaging the hair, can be looked at now with a different scope. Don't get me wrong. I'm not saying that all the damaging practices can now be done. I'm saying that a few techniques that are now permissible as a result of the technology can now be tolerated because they can be rectified and they are the ones that were the least harmful if done regardless. Some techniques are dangerous even now and should not be taken lightly.

Chapter Review

- permanent hair color should be processed for at least 45 minutes

- processing time can be cut down with contraction technology

- relaxing & permanently coloring can be done in the same day with this technology

- hair has to be treated with contraction product after relaxing & again after coloring

- swelling is reduced after each chemical service which allows it to be done the same day

- room temperature processing for color is at 72 degrees

- by placing the client under a cap the processing temperature goes up to about 94 degrees

- by placing the client under a dryer the processing temperature goes up to about 112 degrees

- placing a client under a cap cuts the processing time down from 45 min to about 22 min

- placing a client under a dryer cuts the processing time down from 22 min to about 12 min

- cutting the processing time down like this is okay but should be treated with the contraction product after

7

HISTORY MAKING STEPS IN CONDITIONING

Through all the previous chapters, we have been discussing modern technology and industry breaking information at its best. They have all been topics of a conditioning nature to say the least. However, there is still more developments to be introduced and considered when attempting to become well rounded as a hair care specialist. For decades as I have worked around the country and the world for that matter, I have listened to manufacturers, product companies and chemists talk about how great their respective products are. As I performed as a platform artist, director and consultant for some of these prestigious companies, I have gotten a first hand view of how things are done. Every company insists that their product is better than the next and that they have a little something special that the other doesn't have. There is one attribute that many companies and chemists claim that I've come to understand more and more since studying and working with this new technology that we have been discussing in the previous chapters.

How many times have you attended a class or workshop for a major manufacturing company and they lectured extensively on how their product penetrates the hair shaft and gets deep into the cortex of the hair? I know that I have listened to many speeches on this level. They all contend that their conditioners and treatments penetrate the shaft and get deep into the structure of the hair. As a result of working with the scientists from the hospital and universities, I have learned and confirmed that as far as we all know to this day and time, every conditioner and treatment known to man is oil based to some degree. This includes products designed for Caucasian hair as well as African American hair. These oil based products are not designed or structured to penetrate the hair simply because of its makeup or composition. This is common knowledge and common sense. We know as we have been taught over the years that the molecular structure of oil is too large to penetrate the hair shaft. Since all the products out there on the market are oil based, it would seem pretty obvious and elementary that none of them will do what they claim to do. Many if not all of these products have a characteristic or action that causes them to cling to the hair or attach themselves to the hair and therefore give you the illusion or impression that they are actually penetrating the shaft. They become affixed so we tend to think or are led to believe that they have penetrated the shaft because they haven't left the hair and because they have now changed the reaction of he hair as a result of being attached. Therefore, chemists and product makers insist that these conditioners are indeed getting inside of the hair. This has been the misconception and most misleading of the century.

I instruct my students and attendees of my seminars and workshops to return to the salon and examine the products they use and analyze the ingredients in those products. These products include shampoos, blowdrying lotions, conditioners and treatments alike. I instruct the readers of this book to do the same. Look at the ingredients on the back of these products. Many if not practically all of them have an ingredient in them name PQ or Polyquatenerium. This product has a unique and specific responsibility and quality. It consists of a two sided molecule. One molecular side which is the positive ion side attaches itself to the negative which is the hair and the negative ion attaches itself to water. This gives the characteristic and result of exclusively conditioned hair with noticeable attributes. These attributes are unlike others and exceptional to others. This characteristic warrants the makers and companies to acclaim that their products are doing things unusual and things that ordinary products won't or can't do. They are not deceiving you by saying this. These specific products are indeed exceptional and have a unique and special quality. They are the cream of the best crop as far as conditioners and treatments are concerned as of today. Even with the new technology I'm introducing, they are still quality products. However, they are not doing what the companies are professing. The fact still remains that every conditioner out on the market is oiled based. They have their own exclusive level of oil. So as I instruct you to look carefully at the ingredients on the containers, you will identify that these products that the companies are insisting to penetrate the hair shaft are the very same products that contain the ingredient PQ or polyquaternerium. As I mentioned in chapters previously, we have no real proven procedure or methods of proving otherwise because we have never been in a position educationally to dispute what the manufacturers are saying. We take them at their word. As far as we are concern, this does not necessarily mean that they set out deliberately to deceive us when they make these claims. Let's give them the benefit of the doubt. I would like to think that the manufacturers are supplying us with this specific education simply because based on our intelligence and education level, we perceive the action of the conditioners as actual penetration. In other words, this is the only way that most of us would comprehend the explanation of the work the conditioners are doing. I'm not saying that we as stylists are dumbfounded, but I am saying that most of us don't make a good and accurate analogy of molecular talk and all the logic of molecules when it comes to products and how they work in relation to the hair shaft. So therefore, when the manufacturers tell us this information, they are informing us in a manner in which we can understand and relate.

Before we go any further and explain more accomplished technology, let me explain more of why these PQ based products can only do but so much. The hair has about 5 to 6 layers of cuticle on each strand of hair. We like to call them cells. Each one of those 5 to 6 layers are composed of 4 parts. So now you have as many as 6 cells all composed of 4 inner substances that now start to multiply and ultimately give us a sense of how much cuticle is there and how hard it is to penetrate through it. These 4 parts make up what we call the exo-cuticle, endo-cuticle, the cell membrane and the "A" layer. The exo-cuticle is the outer layer, the endo-cuticle is an inner layer, the cell membrane is a very subtle layer and the "A" layer is the very hard layer. The "A" layer is the layer that is described as the table top hard layer as in the hard substance that make up the nail on your fingers. All these sections have to be pierced and penetrated before you can officially say that a substance has penetrated it. A product that has polyquartenerium in it merely secures itself on the surface. This product clings to the hair and stays there until it is removed with a shampoo or some other service. It leaves the hair very soft because the oils are attached and gives the hair an improved feel. So in reality, these products were indeed the cream of the crop when it came to conditioning. It was supreme to what was formerly available and so when it came about, it was definitely an improvement to previous technology.

Now we have gone even a step further. Now there is finally technology that can actually penetrate the hair shaft. This technology can hold eight times the water than those products containing PQ (polyquaternerium). These molecules not only hold more water but they have been super charged which means they are made very active. This conditioner penetrates the shaft and drags along a great portion of water when it goes in. These conditioners are water based. Water is the thinnest substance you can put into the hair. It gives great cooperation when trying to penetrate because of its molecular size. Due to its molecular composition and characteristics, it has been tested and found beneficial to hair coloring technology. As I mentioned in a previous chapter, there is theory that supports minimizing the processing time in a haircoloring procedure and now there is scientific proof that adding a water based conditioner such as the one I've been describing here now, can intensify and enrich color placement. Let me explain.

Permanent hair color is usually applied to dry hair. Semi-permanent color can be applied in different ways. Now either can be intensified by simply wetting the hair and applying this technology to the hair in small quantities and then apply the color along with it. Since this type of product has the ability to penetrate the shaft, it has super charged qualities as well and it drags color inside with it it's penetration. This strengthens the color application and enriches the look. Now you have good color education, good color products and finally you have understanding and procedures to get that color deep inside the shaft where it can really do some good for the clients. All of this education and industry breakthroughs is supported and backed up by writings and documentaries by scientists in the science world. These writings are built and based on facts.

Chapter Review

- Currently all of your conditioners today are oil based therefore not able to penetrate the shaft

- All of the conditioners out here today have PQ (poly quartenerium) in them

- PQ products have what we describe as a two headed molecule (this means it does not penetrate the shaft)

- PQ gives the characteristics similar of those that penetrate the shaft

- It has a positive ion that attracts to the negative (hair) and a negative ion which is attracted to water. Therefore the water with the negative is on 1 side and the positive with the hair is on the other side which causes an attachment with penetrating characteristics

- Hair has about 5 to 6 layers of cuticle on each strand

- Scientist refer to them as cells

- Each 5 to 6 layers are composed of 4 parts

- The 4 parts consists of a exo-cuticle, endo-cuticle, cell membrane and an "A" layer

- Exo-cuticle is considered as the outer layer

- Endo-cuticle is considered as the inner layer

- Cell membrane is the very subtle layer

- "A" layer is the very hard layer described as sort of a table top hardness

- All these layers have to be pierced in order for penetration to take place which gives you a sense of how difficult it is for a product to penetrate

8

A MESSAGE TO THE MANUFACTURERS

After carefully processing all the materials, documents and discoveries by the science world, I took a careful observation of what the cosmetology industry has been exposed to. Manufacturers have given us the best of the best. They have provided the crème de la crème to the industry for decades. Year after year a different product company arrives to the scene. Each one of them protests that they are first and the last of the quality products that we need. All of the companies available to the industry provide us with great products that we as stylists can make our own and turn into exclusives for our specially tailored clientele. However, none of them stands out apart from the rest. They all have shampoos and conditioners that they insist is the best on the market. They claim all of their conditioners penetrate the hair shaft. The fact of the matter is that many if not most of these products do not do what the manufacturers say. I'm not saying that the manufacturers have been lying to us but I will say that they have given us the best that they could give us and that is all that they were exposed to.

Let's take the situation with the new technology for example. The contracting solution provides something to hairdressing that could not be provided by current manufacturers. This contracting formula does what couldn't be done before. It contracts the swelling in the hair that comes from chemicals and heat. Manufacturers have been telling us for years that their products penetrate the shaft and provide the necessary conditioning that is required in order to leave the hair in a healthy state. I'm not sure if they really felt that their products penetrated the inner shaft of the hair or if they knew it wasn't possible. The fact is that hair stylists around the world saw a proportionate level of success with these products and as far as they were concerned, there wasn't any better alternative. We felt that we had the best products around. Each one of us had our exclusive pick of products and we adjusted to what they could do or not do. As an educator, I have always felt that the products that were available to us were in close proximity of one another and the difference in them came with the ability of the user. I always said that the product is only as good as the user. So a skilled stylist could take his craft and abilities and make an average product above average. In chapters previous, I mentioned details about ingredients in products that dispute the penetration of the hair shaft. Manufacturers knew this. They knew what their products could do and what they couldn't. However, the level of comprehension between the stylists and manufacturers is a little demented. We have a limited amount of education when it comes to product knowledge. Even though most stylists would swim through a pool of sharks to get to a product class, they have little or no understanding of what the manufacturers are providing to us. We are easily deceived and gullible. Most of us believe anything that is told to us. If a manufacturer tells us that their product penetrates the shaft, we will believe it with no questions asked. Therefore manufacturers have had the luxury of making their presentations with little or no friction.

As I mentioned in previous chapters, hair breakage is contributed to one major factor and that is swelling. As of today, none of the companies have developed a reverse procedure for this swelling. A solution to this problem would set one company apart from the rest. Even though the manufacturers knew that they were not reducing the swelling in the hair, they still protested that they were solving the damage and breakage problems plaguing so much of the industry. In a sense they were deceiving us. They knew that those products weren't doing all that they were claiming them to do. On the other hand, here is where the problem manifested. Stylists were using these products from all these companies that were claiming that they were doing things that they weren't. All they knew is that there was significant progress in the hair. The hair was being softened as a result of some of these conditioners. Some of the treatments by these companies were actually making the hair feel better. Unfortunately, all of these products were not penetrating the hair shaft as they were labeled as doing, but instead they were sitting and resting on the outside of the hair giving characteristics of products that could penetrate. As I mentioned before, no products known to us currently actually penetrated the shaft anyway. So we had no real way of knowing what the attributes or characteristics of those types of products were anyway. So instead of knowing the facts, we were misled into believing that the characteristics that we were seeing were indeed those of products with ingredients capable of penetrating the shaft. We thought we had the best. Scientists proved that every product out here on the conditioning side is oil based and therefore cannot penetrate the cuticle. They proved that all these so called penetrating products were actually attaching themselves to the shaft and thus giving them characteristics of penetrating solutions. Manufacturers of today still insist that their products do specific and unusual things. They still insist that a neutralizing shampoo is necessary and appropriate for relaxer services. They still maintain the teachings that these shampoos exclusively do the business of removing and stopping the chemical action in the hair from sodium hydroxide relaxers. I've already explained that this can never happen unless the sodium hydroxide is converted into a sodium chloride. No neutralizing shampoo can do this unless it is formulated much different than current and modern technology shampoos of today. It has been proven through science that only a specific kind of product with characteristics and appropriate activity points can successfully achieve this.

The technology of the contracting solution is not the only example of misconceptions manufacturers have given the industry. We are so eager to accept any and everything a manufacturer throws on us that we don't even stop to analyze what we use or even check its merit. Take the gels, spritz and sprays for example. It is obvious what these types of products can do to the hair. It doesn't take a skilled or trained eye to observe the potential threat these types of product can have on the hair but we use them anyway. Manufacturers encourage it. It is all about the money. I propose that manufacturers come up with a shampoo that has the ingredients and attributes of converting a sodium hydroxide into a sodium chloride. After all, shampoos have always been the product that follows the rinsing of the chemical for centuries. So why not create a shampoo that could possess the ability to have enough activity points to successfully and completely convert the sodium hydroxide hair into the salt form that is necessary to remove it. We have always proclaimed that the neutralizing shampoo has the composition to achieve removal of the chemical, so let's just invent technology to impart the exclusive ingredients to make it really do its job.

Another major issue I have with manufacturers of today is the need for quantity as opposed to quality. Many manufacturers of today have as many as thirty six to fifty products in there line. I personally feel that this is entirely too many products. With the increasing and alarming number of companies originating over the years, we have become bombarded with more and more products and not nearly enough knowledge to accompany it. The average stylist today cannot afford to purchase every product in a particular line. I know in all my years as a stylist and educator I have never purchased an entire line exclusively. With the saturation of products out here today, there are many great choices and availabilities for the stylists. I have been all around the world and have taught stylists from all over the world and I don't recall ever finding a particular person who has only one line of products that they use. Most stylists have a particular relaxer that they use along with a couple of shampoos and conditioners. However, there are a large percentage of stylists who use as many as three to four different brands of relaxer. So with that comes a shampoo or two from one line and a shampoo or two from another line. Then there are the products like gels, sprays, lotions etc. These stylists may purchase a gel from one company and sprays and lotions from a couple other companies. The fact of the matter is that with the state of the economy today, there are incidents where the stylists go out and purchase a container of relaxer, a neutralizing shampoo, a conditioning shampoo, a couple of deep conditioners and maybe a setting lotion or blow drying lotion or two and create a ticket of well over $150.00. So can you imagine purchasing products for the week or month and buying all thirty or fifty products in a particular line? This would eat up any and all profit you intend to make. I have said for many years now that it has been strictly about the money with many manufacturers. It's about the marketing of products to accomplish the bottom line. I think it would be more effective for the manufacturers as well as the stylists to develop a small core of products with amazing and phenomenal attributes rather than develop a million products that you know are not going to attract the multitude of the people. A small core of products could be highly concentrated throughout the population with greater effects, than a huge amount of products that would be scattered in small amounts throughout the population. This way, the stylists would make better choices and would be able to develop a higher quality of service with a designated and exclusive line of products. Until this happens, there will continue to be the multitude of the industry buying a few products from this manufacturer and a few products from two or three other manufacturer to develop a complete regimen of service for their clientele.

Chapter Review

Review for this chapter is slightly different than those of previous chapters. Simply apply your own assessments and observations of how you feel the industry is going based on what I've talked about in this chapter and according to how you feel personally. Draw your own personal conclusions before preceding to the final chapter.

9

WHY I CAN'T KEEP QUIET

This chapter is somewhat a personal one for me. It expresses and reveals why it was important for me to do this book and to expose information to the industry that I feel is valuable and necessary. I felt it was necessary for me to open up this can of worms because I feel the very core of the industry is being taken for a ride. This core I'm speaking of is the stylists and the salon businesses. Our stylists are so misled and so misguided that is pathetic. We are sometimes like patients walking out of a physician's office with bags full of medicine with no real comprehension of what they can do and the harm they can cause when misused. As I implied in the previous chapter, we have tons and tons of products at our disposal. We have more products than we can handle and more products than we have an understanding of. We have these products but we don't have the education that should be accompanied with it. I'm in the classroom two to three times a month in cities all over the nation. As long as I have been teaching, I still have many students that are amazed at the information that they receive and amazed at how much they didn't know. You would think it would come full circle by now but there are a million people out here in the industry that still have not received the valuable information that they need. So when I see the alarming number of individuals that need such valuable information, it makes it hard for me as an educator to sit by and say nothing. I want to arm my fellow stylists with the most effective weapon they could ever possess and that is education. We have always been so consumed up with product knowledge that we don't put enough emphasis on technical service. All we have is a bunch of products and no understanding of how to use them. Manufacturers have platform artists on their stages but there is little education for the stylists that really want to know. Our stylists go on the tradeshow floor and gather up all the information from the manufacturers that they want you to have but they never come to the classroom to get the whole truth.

I have been to all kinds of shows from all parts of the country. I've seen manufacturers put up sponsorship money for tradeshows and lately I've seen more manufacturers putting up money for competitions. More and more companies are sponsoring competitions. Many of them are putting up tens of thousands of dollars. Stylists are coming out of the woodwork to participate in these extravagant competitions. The result is large numbers of individuals with no experience in hair care and no real knowledge of how things work, with thousands of dollars in their pockets that gives them attitudes and chips on their shoulders the size of watermelons. These stylists develop cocky attitudes that become blocked from allowing any guidance or direction from trained individuals in the education world.

I challenge manufacturers to sponsor an educator. What's wrong with that? Why not sponsor one of us? They put up money all the time and sometimes taking a massive loss as a result. They have platform artist on their stages that are supposed to be teaching for them, so why not put some of that investment into some of the premier educators. The problem is that those platform artists are preaching their praises and their praises only. By any means necessary. As long as the message gets out that their products are supreme and the dollars are being made then their mission is accomplished. Unfortunately, there is a story that is not being told on the platform stage. There are truths that are not being exposed. I feel that most of them believe or fear that we as educators will hurt their ability to sell products. If the truth be told, there is a lot of good that the educators could provide for the manufacturers. We have much more control over the bottom line than they realize. We could help the companies sell twice as many products as they do if they would only wake up and realize where the real worth of this industry is. There are insights that we as educators provide that no other entity provides. If we had the support of the manufacturers in the form of sponsorship money like that of the money that they give to the competitions, we could change the industry. Manufacturers don't encourage stylists to visit the classrooms. We teach sound education on technical services such as cutting, roller placement, chemical relaxing, coloring, styling techniques and more. Without these classes, the products wouldn't mean much. Without this type of training, the products would provide little exclusivity. This is what sets us apart from the rest. We arm ourselves with knowledge and education on the subjects and in turn it makes us superior in the industry to those who are not educated. It really means something when you hear that famous cliché of, "a mind is a terrible thing to waste". Instead we continue to go by the tradeshow floor and listen to a few words of wisdom from the platform artists and then make a big purchase only to move on to the next vendor and do the same. All the while they have not received an ounce of education.

As I mentioned in a previous chapter, the manufacturers are becoming so large in terms of the quantity of products they have that they have spread out their inventory in a very thin way. Now more than ever they are adding more and more products to their line in hopes of increasing their bottom line. Many of them now are adding a color line to their arsenal. They are trying to saturate the market. I don't know about the majority but I would prefer to buy my colors from a color manufacturer as opposed to a manufacturer that specializing in chemical relaxers. You wouldn't want to buy your shirts from an automobile dealer would you? You wouldn't want to buy your groceries from a beauty supply would you? Neither would I. Unfortunately, many stylists don't register with this concept. We are very gullible when it comes to buying products. We can be sold on almost anything a manufacturer gives us. Since we don't have the education about color, it is sometimes hard for us to understand and realize that color is a delicate subject and that their best choices and results are going to come from a color manufacturer. The more we know, the more effective we are as buyers and as stylists.

Finally, I see something that gives me no choice but to scream murder. I see an empire of an industry crumbling before me. That industry is the black beauty industry. For years now, I see more and more tradeshows falling by the way side. I see more and more stylists coming to shows and never stopping by the classroom. I see more and more black product manufacturers leaving black hair shows and going into the Caucasian tradeshows. At the same time, I see more and more Caucasian tradeshow companies putting up shows all over the nation on almost a monthly basis. They are in the same business as we are and they seem to be growing in paramount ways. However, we are regressing and going further and further in the whole. I see my industry failing at progress. We as educators are not getting the respect that we deserve and are not getting our due. I have a strong following and it is my mission to inform my people. Don't get me wrong. It is not about color or race. It is all about preserving an industry whether white or black. However, I don't see the white side of the industry ailing. So it is my intentions to build the industry back up by providing information. This information is coming in the form of education. I want to give this industry all the insides of this business and help strengthen the stylists into more effective professionals by increasing their information base. Meanwhile, I again challenge manufacturers to sponsor an educator. Put the money where it can be most effective. Their sponsorship dollars will go ten times farther invested in an educator as opposed to a competition. Entertainment is alright but we are not in the entertainment business. We are in the haircare business. The caliber of education that I and my peers provide is not going to come from the tradeshow stage. The only way I know how to ensure what the industry needs is to provide them with the information that the companies don't provide. So in essence, I am like an extension of the manufacturers. I inform and teach the stylists how to better use the products and how to get the most of what they pay for. In addition, I won't sugar coat it by harboring valuable information that will also bring harm to the integrity of the hair. I'm going to keep on doing what I do as long as the manufacturers continue to do what they do.

978-0-595-45272-9
0-595-45272-8